THE WORKPLACE TRANSFRMED

7 CRUCIAL LESSONS FROM THE GLOBAL PANDEMIC

Moving Beyond Covid-19 and
Embracing the New Future of Work

ANGELA J. REDDOCK-WRIGHT, ESQ.

The Workplace Transformed: 7 Crucial Lessons from The Global Pandemic

Copyright © 2022 by Angela J. Reddock-Wright

All rights reserved.

Published by Red Penguin Books

Bellerose Village, New York

Library of Congress Control Number: 2022902439

ISBN

Print 978-1-63777-215-7

Digital 978-1-63777-216-4

No part of this book may be reproduced in any form or by any electronic or mechanical means, including information storage and retrieval systems, without written permission from the author, except for the use of brief quotations in a book review.

This book is dedicated to

All employees, essential workers and individuals who have worked on the frontlines throughout the COVID-19 pandemic, and during one of the most harrowing times in world history. From healthcare professionals to grocery store workers, to retail employees and public transportation operators – you have been here for us when we needed you most.

All businesses, organizations and employers who have demonstrated remarkable flexibility and incredible resilience in the face of unprecedented challenges, and found new ways to move forward, while encouraging, empowering, and lifting up their employees and turning calamity into success. Thank you to both employees and employers alike for making the ultimate sacrifice and braving the pandemic to continue servicing our communities.

Those who have experienced substantial physical, mental, emotional, and final hardship during these times.

Those who have lost loved ones and who have been at the center of caregiving for their loved ones.

This book is a reminder that every person has value and that some of the most devastating and heart wrenching crises can bring out the best in people and transform both lives and workplaces, as long as we continue to rise to the occasion and grow from the lessons learned.

CONTENTS

Introduction — vii

1. Elevating HR to a Higher Ground — 1

2. Employee Engagement: Building Your Best Team Yet — 15

3. COVID-19's Impact on Essential Workers, Women and Minorities — 25

4. The Rising Wave of Employee Activism — 33

5. Daily Commute No More? Avoiding the Grind and Escaping Rush Hour Traffic — 43

6. The Importance of Disaster Preparedness and Crisis Prevention — 51

7. Discerning Legal Challenges and Changes — 59

Conclusion — 67

Acknowledgments — 71

About the Author — 75

"Wait--how many seasons is this?"

INTRODUCTION

"History, despite its wrenching pain, cannot be unlived, but if faced with courage, need not be lived again."
- Maya Angelou

In this beautifully poignant quote, world-renowned poet and author Maya Angelou reflects on how important it is to learn from our past: as individuals and as a society. In fact, it couldn't be timelier and more relevant to what we are going through right now. In the past two years of enduring the COVID-19 pandemic, we have lived through one of the toughest times in recent history. Many of us vaguely remember how it all started...

Back when we learned about the outbreak of a "mysterious pneumonia" in China in December 2019, little did we know how far the disease would spread and the devastating impact it would have all around the world. The World Health Organization declared COVID-19 a pandemic in March 2020, and it's safe to say that very few of us have ever anticipated such a dramatic turn of events or expected to witness such an epic loss of life – about 6.3 million people to date and counting.

As for me, never could I have imagined I would become part of the solution and write a book that documents valuable lessons learned as the world was forced to evolve, adapt, and transform over a short period of time - faster, in fact, than we could have ever envisioned.

There are a few main reasons I decided to write this book and share my insights with the world. Of course, we are all aware that the pandemic devastated our economy, disrupting the job market and overwhelming our healthcare system while pushing essential workers beyond their physical and mental limits. Without a doubt, observing the myriad of challenges, caused by this global health crisis, has been heartbreaking.

Yet, at the same time, the whole experience has given me hope, even in the darkest of moments, and made me realize that adversity may serve as a powerful force to push things forward. It can fuel positive change and improve different aspects of our lives, both on personal and professional levels. In other words, I am hoping that this book will inspire my readers and serve as a reminder that, sometimes, out of bad comes something good.

In addition to that, I have to admit my nature has always been to avidly watch and learn. As a former employment and labor law litigator turned mediator, arbitrator, and investigator, my passion is to observe how employers and employees interact and achieve progress. As a result, I closely follow all the new developments and trends that cause key short-term and long-term changes to the world of work. I have certainly paid particular attention to how living through COVID-19 has fundamentally altered the "traditional" 21st century work environment.

In this book I stress how childcare disruptions, the shuttering of so many businesses and offices, and the expansion of our virtual world has transformed the way we communicate, engage with one another, and manage employees, among other things.

Furthermore, while some workplaces are getting back to business, and many others are carefully planning to follow suit and get back into the swing of things, employees are increasingly resisting or challenging the status quo. Evidence suggests that they want their employers to respond to ever-evolving needs and concerns that affect both individuals and the company as a whole: motivation, productivity, race relations, compensation and support in the workplace, and many other crucial issues that still need to be addressed.

Coincidentally, as I sit here writing this intro in the wake of the 20th anniversary of the September 11th terrorist attacks, I find myself drawing parallels in my mind between 2001 and 2020 – two years of tragedy, uncertainty, and adjustment. While it may be impossible to directly compare 9/11 and COVID-19, one thing is for sure: it is vital to document where we have been, no matter how dramatic, especially as we live through historic events that irreversibly alter the world as we once knew it. It bears repeating that these milestones become lessons learned that enable us to grow, improve ourselves, and gain strength in the face of adversity. That's what this book is all about.

Each one of us can reflect on how these events have shaped our own lives and altered our attitudes. That's why my goal for this book is to reflect upon and create a dialogue around some of the major transformations the pandemic has brought about in my sphere of influence: the world of work. Even more importantly, I'd like to challenge us all to contemplate where we go from here, and what lessons we can carry forward into an uncertain future while maintaining a positive outlook.

The lessons briefly outlined below serve as a summary of the book stressing the issues, the lessons learned, and the solutions for better, brighter, and safer times ahead. I am convinced it's a worthwhile endeavor that will make a difference and help companies and their employees navigate the "new normal" with confidence.

Lessons Learned from the Pandemic:
The 4Es and the 3Ds to Keep in Mind for Years to Come

In light of current events, I am happy to share my insights in a book that captures the essence of the drastic changes caused by the crushing pandemic. These changes caught us off guard, influencing every aspect of our lives. Yet, I also believe that unexpected challenges may lead to opportunities, as every disaster or emergency offers lessons learned as well as a chance for employers and employees, alike, to prepare for future crises.

Furthermore, as a seasoned mediator and alternative dispute resolution professional, I believe that every perspective, every opinion and individual voice may potentially be of value and should be seriously considered. Each person, family, organization, or group of people have faced the challenges of the pandemic in a unique way. Notably, over the past two years, we have seen how traditionally undervalued voices have been ignored or taken for granted. Essential workers, in particular, who were expected to carry a heavy burden for the rest of us, have so much to teach us and serve as a reminder about who steps up to the plate in a time of crisis. That's something each one of us should keep in mind going forward.

While reading this book, you will come across many examples of serious drawbacks and stressors facing employers and their employees. You will also get to read about some innovative solutions being explored that turned some difficulties into opportunities, transforming a bad situation into a good one.

For easier reference, I have divided the chapter themes into **the 4Es** and **3Ds**. From *elevating* human resources, *engaging* employees, supporting *essential* workers, responding to *employee* protests and activism (4Es), to unveiling alternatives to the *daily* commute, developing *disaster* preparedness plans, and *discerning* legal challenges (3Ds), I delve into the work-related issues that have been on everyone's mind since the onset of the pandemic in 2020.

My intention is to demonstrate empathy for employers and employees alike, while conveying useful, timely, and relevant insights that will help both parties successfully navigate and prepare as the workplace landscape continues to rapidly evolve.

We have lost so much over the course of the global pandemic. Sadly, as I write this, the suffering has not yet ended, and we have yet to figure out what the future holds. That said, I believe many of us have gained a whole lot more than we lost. I am looking forward to showing you how.

To your success,
Angela

1

ELEVATING HR TO A HIGHER GROUND

Let's face it: the global pandemic was an unexpected calamity that turned our lives upside down and forced us to shift our priorities. It created a myriad of setbacks, challenges and obstacles, both in our personal and professional lives, that need to be addressed. That said, I strongly believe that every disaster has a silver lining providing opportunities to grow and lessons to be learned.

In some organizations, the issues that have been on the backburner, for too long, have skyrocketed to the forefront as a result of the pandemic. Companies that fail to adjust and step up to the plate are in for a rude awakening. The urgency is real and the stakes have never been higher. This brings us to the newly found power of HR in the post-COVID era.

Now, let's examine some major obstacles confronting HR and revisit lessons learned from the global pandemic.

When Obstacles Arise, All Eyes Are on HR

DEALING WITH THE HEARTBREAK OF WORKPLACE REDUCTIONS

During the pandemic, many organizations have been forced to cut their expenses and shed jobs, tasking HR with the heart-wrenching responsibility of addressing furloughs, layoffs and workforce reductions. At a time of unexpected upheaval, remaining employees may experience enormous stress and feel insecure in their jobs. After all, who is next to go? We all agree that job insecurity may take a toll on employee well-being and mental health and make a bad situation worse. Without a doubt, it can be demotivating and potentially discourage workers from giving their best to their employer. It means that HR should find new ways to communicate with employees, provide regular support, and demonstrate deeper appreciation for workers.

HARNESSING WORKPLACE ENGAGEMENT

As organizations switched to remote work, keeping employees engaged, motivated, and inspired is no easy feat. Let's face it: it's so much harder to manage a big group of people when you can't watch, supervise or manage them directly. Besides, so many folks working from home may feel isolated and can easily get distracted, which may impact their morale and impede productivity. The question is: how do HR specialists ensure everyone is on the same page, working together as a team, and functioning to the best of their ability? In addition, it is essential that all teams across the organization fully-understand and comply with company policies. That's where a strategic communications plan comes into play to help HR maintain contact with all workers and make them feel like their presence is critical to organizational success.

STATUS QUO NO MORE: THE URGENT NEED TO MODIFY WORKING ARRANGEMENTS

While adjusting to remote work is still a "work in progress," HR should also embrace the hybrid model and offer workers the flexibility that they need to achieve job satisfaction. Striking the right balance could be a challenge, yet it is also an opportunity to improve employee well-being. By the way, Gartner research reveals that 48% of workers will work remotely at least part of the time after the pandemic, compared with 30% before COVID-19.

CASTING YOUR NET FAR AND WIDE: TAPPING INTO A BIGGER TALENT POOL

Now that face-to-face interviews are becoming a thing of the past, many companies are struggling to embrace new technologies that allow them to attract, carefully screen, and onboard top talent. Even during the best of times, nabbing the right job candidates is a challenge. At first glance, "cherry picking" the right people in the post-pandemic world seems like an insurmountable task. Now, more than ever, HR leaders must build their technical acumen and use innovative technologies to successfully address this new undertaking.

RACE AGAINST TIME TO FINE-TUNE COMPANY CULTURE

Another major challenge confronting the "old personnel department" is upgrading or recreating company culture. According to research findings published by the Harvard Business Review, cultural adaptability reflects every organization's ability to innovate, experiment, and benefit from new opportunities. This is especially important at this historic moment.

There is a whole lot for HR to figure out when it comes to culture: should companies become more transparent, is there a way to build trust and connect with team members on a deeper level while working from home? Furthermore, would it be enough to upgrade internal rules and regulations, or is it necessary to replace them with new ones? There are so many questions but so little time - while everyone is looking to HR to deliver solutions.

"UPSKILLING" EMPLOYEES TO REMAIN COMPETITIVE

Pandemic or not, the business world continues to evolve rapidly and this means that employees' skills should evolve with it. It goes without saying that regular training, upleveling, or reskilling of employees should be placed at the top of the priority list. But training and educating workers who operate from home can be tricky, and for obvious reasons. Once again, it is incumbent on HR folks to introduce new technologies that can facilitate remote learning, clearly communicate the importance of new skill-sets, and set expectations. With a structured approach, it will be easier to educate employees and hold them accountable for results.

As you can see, challenges abound, and the laundry list of new tasks has no end in sight. But we can't talk about obstacles without stressing the importance of lessons driven by the global pandemic. Now, let's review the critical pointers below, roll up our sleeves, and get to work.

Key Lessons Learned from HR in 2020

1. LEADERSHIP FROM THE TOP

In the post-pandemic world, it is clear that employees expect to see leadership from the top. Gone are the days where executives and CEOs can hide behind glass walls and corner offices. Their teams are expecting them to be at the forefront and leading by example. Despite overwhelming schedules, every executive should become more accessible, more involved, and make an extra effort to pull their teams together - especially at this time when their leadership is needed the most. Failure to break the barriers may discourage workers, create a disconnect, and potentially send things spinning out of control. Alternatively, keeping everyone together leads to trust, mutual respect, and enhanced performance. Those in leadership roles should clearly communicate with managers and staff and fully-commit to employee health and well-being.

2. BUSINESS SURVIVAL 101: RUNNING A MISSION AND VALUES DRIVEN ORGANIZATION

I think business professionals would agree that an organization, without a clearly-articulated mission and strong values, is not ready to navigate the post-covid environment. Every executive, in collaboration with HR, should invest time and effort into enhancing and redefining corporate culture.

When it comes to cultural upgrade, it is not only existing employees who need to be kept in the loop. The "new hires" boarding the big ship should be adequately educated about the corporate culture and embrace their employer's biggest goals, needs, and aspirations.

Closing the gap between an existing and desired "state of affairs" is not easy. No pressure, HR folks! Just keep in mind that companies with a strong and well-defined culture, will be the ones that have the ammunition to weather the storm and come out on top *(according to research out of University of California, Berkeley's Haas School of Business)*. In fact, organizations with a positive corporate culture tend to perform 15% better than those who failed to adapt.

3. IMAGINATION TO THE RESCUE: GETTING CREATIVE WITH WORKING ARRANGEMENTS

As the saying goes, "variety is the spice of life." In other words, HR professionals should get creative when it comes to designing a variety of work arrangements that may increase job satisfaction.

While many workers miss regular watercooler chats and daily bonding with their colleagues, regular communications, emails, phone calls, and video chats will ensure that everyone is on the same wavelength and that no one feels abandoned or isolated from the rest of the team. Will it replace daily office interactions? Probably not. However, various studies show that remote workers have been more productive, which is a result that business executives tend to welcome, along with lower office space costs.

Interestingly, many millennials prefer the hybrid or dispersed model, including suburban satellite offices, that allow them to achieve a highly-desired work/life balance. This type of arrangement is also welcomed by women with young children, who are intent on reentering the job market after the pandemic.

4. STATING THE OBVIOUS: THE COMPANY IS AS GOOD AS ITS EMPLOYEES

The upshot of the prolonged pandemic is that business leaders have come to realize the increased importance of a strong, cohesive, and happy workforce. In other words, hardworking team members can no longer be taken for granted or treated as easily-disposable units. Why? Simple. Each organization is only as good as the people working for it. Therefore, business leaders and HR professionals should join in their efforts to motivate, encourage, and inspire employees and show a deeper appreciation for their input.

By the way, it is important to keep in mind that a tighter labor market gives workers more leverage with employers. Even lower-end service workers are empowered to request signing bonuses, higher wages, and more humane working conditions. While the unemployment rate is over 6%, and the country had 8 million fewer positions in March of 2021 (as stated by the Los Angeles Times), there is still a growing shortage of workers and more than 7 million unfilled jobs. The reason I am sharing these statistics is to demonstrate, once more, how important it is to incentivize employees and never take their contributions for granted.

To corroborate my point about the importance of engaging employees, I am sharing the following statistical data: According to Gallup data from 2017, "highly engaged business units" saw a 41% absenteeism reduction, a 17% increase in productivity, and a 21% increase in profitability. Notably, Gallup described some key elements of engagement, including empowering employees to utilize their talents, clarifying expectations, utilizing employee feedback, and including development initiatives.

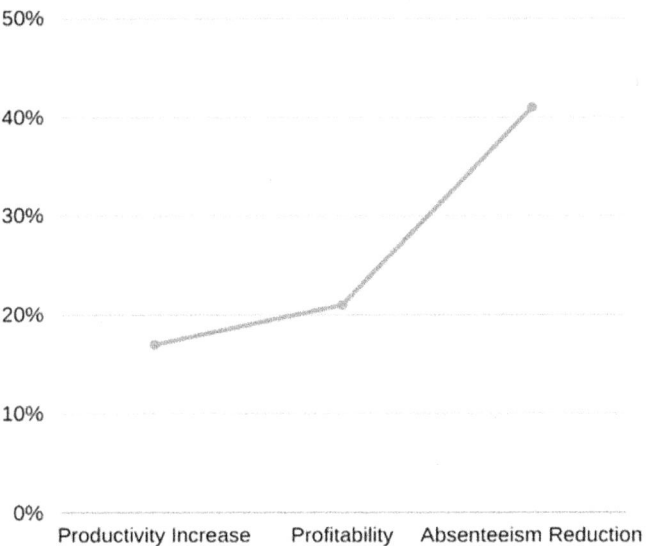

Now let's pay a quick visit to UPS, the company that helps its workers realize their career dreams through part-time work and tuition assistance. Interestingly, UPS employees can earn up to $25,000 for their college education.

Another great example is Chipotle Mexican Grill, which is helping its employees narrow the skills gap through personal development tools and online education.

5. GETTING TO THE CORE: PLACING DIVERSITY, EQUITY & INCLUSION (DEI) AT THE CENTER OF COMPANY STRATEGY

The past year has taught us the significance of addressing workforce inequality among women, people of color, and the under-served communities. This is what will make our organizations more resilient in the face of adversity.

According to research provided by KPMG, a survey of employees at more than 1,700 companies in eight countries and across all industries, revealed that companies with more diverse teams achieved 19% higher revenues due to innovation and a variety of creative ideas. Additionally, a study of profitable organizations in 91 countries, by the Peterson Institute for International Economics, indicated that companies with a 30% representation of female leaders attained a 15% increase in their net revenue margins. These are the numbers that organizations and HR leaders can no longer ignore.

There is another interesting finding. The L.A. Times states that people of color will comprise half of the working class by 2032. Therefore, now more than ever, it is important to put more emphasis on diversity, equity, and inclusion and make sure everyone's voice is being heard, considered, and appreciated.

People of color will comprise half the working class by 2032

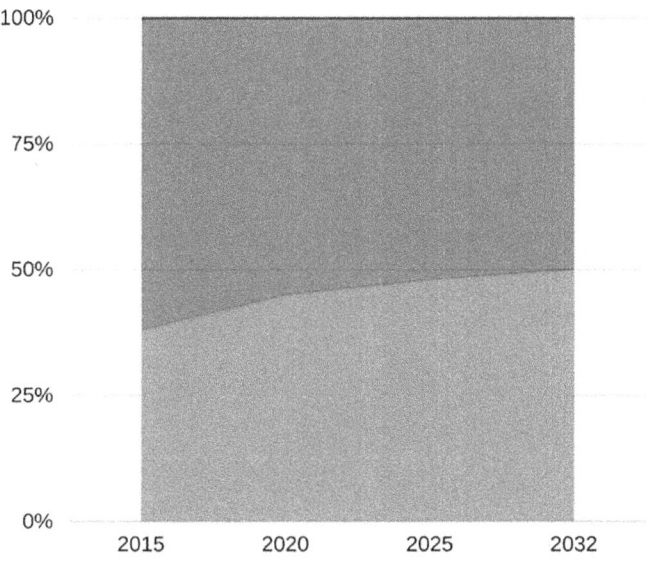

6. MOVING FORWARD FULL SPEED AHEAD

As we progress beyond the pandemic, we have a myriad of opportunities to move the most crucial workplace issues from the back burner to the spotlight. As we find better ways to foster diversity, well-being, and high motivation, we move from recovery mode into the creation of a more fair, productive, and uplifting workplace – a much better alternative to the status quo.

While transition is rarely easy, companies, organizations, and workers stand to gain. It goes without saying that HR leaders have their work cut out for them. By embracing pivotal leadership roles and closely collaborating with business executives, they have the power to transform their organizations, bring out the best in their employees, and create an amazing workplace – remote, hybrid, or any other shape it may take. Indeed, we may be witnessing the golden age of HR.

"I never thought I'd see the day, they're taking our ideas seriously at last!"

2

EMPLOYEE ENGAGEMENT: BUILDING YOUR BEST TEAM YET

When it comes to adjusting to the "new normal" in the workplace, the pandemic has taught us so much. One of the things we have come to realize is that a strong organization is more than just sales, revenues and dollar figures plastered across the spreadsheets. Forbes suggests that the connection between employees and their company plays a huge role in how successful the business actually is and how profitable it will be in the future. Additionally, organizations that prevail and thrive, despite the unprecedented challenges caused by COVID-19, deeply appreciate the teams that drive their success. They constantly look for new ways to engage, encourage and inspire their workers and provide all the tools they need to maximize their potential. The interesting example below underscores the importance of employee engagement and its impact on employee morale, efficiency, and creativity.

Let's start off by using our imagination…

Imagine what daily life might be like at a company where employee engagement and enthusiasm are more important than rules or processes. As an engaged employee, you would utilize your strengths and talents to the fullest, taking responsibility for your actions and the resulting outcomes. Workers at all levels CAN and DO make crucial decisions that may benefit the whole team and propel their organization forward. Work flexibility is no longer a privilege granted to few, but a way of life afforded to every employee. At decision-making meetings, you feel empowered to express your point of view or voice your concerns and an appointed team leader, also known as a "captain," embraces dissent, considers a wide variety of opinions, ideas, and suggestions, and ultimately proceeds to make an informed judgment call. Additionally, the CEO, who is amenable to your ideas, may regularly solicit your feedback and deeply appreciate your unique perspective.

Sounds too good to be true? Believe it or not, the company I've been telling you about actually exists, and I bet you've heard of it. I'm talking about Netflix, the groundbreaking video streaming giant with a dedicated webpage that thoroughly explains the company culture to prospective job candidates. According to Glassdoor, over 70% of employees would recommend Netflix to others as a potential employer and a great place to work. That being said, the company's "dream team" philosophy has its drawbacks. Employee engagement is literally a "must," since "merely adequate" performers receive a "generous severance package." Furthermore, while the company claims that every individual is encouraged to regularly provide honest, constructive feedback, some people of color may feel more hesitant than their Caucasian counterparts to openly express their concerns to the higher-ups, as suggested by a *Wall Street Journal* investigation conducted in 2018. It is common sense that feeling disenfranchised may potentially discourage workers from putting their best foot forward, contributing to the best of their ability, and spreading the good word about their employer.

The above example corroborates a widely-established notion that in today's digital world, the importance of employee engagement cannot be overstated, and a company is only as good as its engaged personnel. Workplace well-being matters, especially during turbulent times. More than ever before, employers are being held accountable for the work environment they foster.

As a result of the pandemic, the challenges we've faced have led to some valuable lessons that may serve us well - even after the current health crisis ends.

Employee Engagement Challenges

Adapting to the Virtual World

While some people had already grown accustomed to video chatting before the pandemic, others had to learn the ins and outs of Zoom and other virtual meeting platforms in a hurry. As we all know, when it comes to technology, occasional malfunctioning, computer glitches and software failures are inevitable, impeding productivity and creating even more stress for employers and employees, alike. On top of that, remote working has given rise to Zoom-Bombing, the practice of "unwanted guests" intruding on Zoom meetings for malicious purposes. As stated in Newsweek, the FBI issued a warning about potential hijacking and put out a press release about multiple reports of online conferences being disrupted by hate images, threatening language, or obscene messages.

Furthermore, there is another issue that has become quite prevalent due to increased use of video conferencing during the pandemic. We have all heard a multitude of stories where Zoom participants have let their guard down and inadvertently embarrassed themselves in front of their colleagues, bosses, and clients, or even in front of the whole world. Remember the highly-bizarre and widely-publicized incident involving Jeffrey Toobin (a critically-acclaimed journalist and TV personality) and his fall from grace during a video conference, which subsequently went viral and ruined his reputation? As a result, the hashtag #MeToobin spread fast, as people started posting stories online revealing their own moments of shame.

In addition to the potentially embarrassing incidents described above, camera shyness may abound during online encounters with anxious employees suffering the most. In fact, evidence suggests that a lot of workers feel apprehensive about how they look on screen and struggle to achieve the most "presentable" look.

What about women in particular? It's no secret that women have always felt the pressure to look good. What's more, studies suggest that appearance has been an issue for women who are struggling to adjust to Zoom, Webex, Skype, Google Hangout, and other online platforms during the pandemic. According to Vox.com, online interactions have "only triggered a virtual backslide on the body positivity front."

There is other new research, from Washington University in St. Louis, primarily focusing its attention on women and exploring how online meetings impact their satisfaction with their appearance. The aforementioned study suggests that prolonged exposure to Zoom may result in "a general feeling of diminished satisfaction" as our video conferencing usage went up. While at this point, body image concerns may not necessarily be at the forefront of an employer's priorities, it is perhaps something to be mindful of, as we are still in the process of embracing the virtualization of our activities. Furthermore, the employee engagement challenge is to handle all these issues and concerns with grace and even some humor (when appropriate), so that meeting attendees will not get too flustered or simply tune-out.

MOTIVATING EXHAUSTED, OVERWORKED EMPLOYEES

As people are moving through the long-drawn-out pandemic and its accompanying restrictions, they are carefully reassessing their jobs and their lives, in general. After all, there's nothing like a harrowing health crisis to hammer home the old adage that "life is short." Some say that we are in the midst of the Great Resignation of 2021, a growing movement where people are quitting their jobs 'en masse.' Job vacancies reached a 20-year high as four million workers walked away from their jobs in April 2021, a 20-year record, according to the U.S. Department of Labor. In June of 2020, the US Chamber of Commerce called the labor shortage a "national economic emergency," as reported by Business Insider.

Once employees have transitioned to working from home and started enjoying and appreciating the quality of their lives' increasing, many may be reluctant to get back to their office jobs. What's more is that the downtime during the pandemic enabled so many people to develop new skill-sets and passions that they are determined to continue to incorporate them into their day-to-day lives. As a result, for many businesses, employee engagement may be one of the most crucial challenges to address as it could potentially threaten company survival.

It appears that we have reached a point where financial incentives or bonuses may no longer be enough to fulfill employees and their rapidly-evolving needs. Instead, many previously complacent workers are starting to seek more well-rounded benefits packages, welcoming company cultures, flexible working arrangements, and educational and growth opportunities. In other words, employees need more than a salary or increased financial rewards; they want to experience greater fulfillment, live a meaningful life, and have the opportunity to make a difference.

CONNECTING, UNITING AND INSPIRING SOCIALLY-ADRIFT EMPLOYEES

Back in the day, working from home and avoiding a daily commute seemed like a dream come true and a blissful existence. Reports suggest that despite some obvious benefits of remote work, many individuals feel isolated and miss casual chats by the coffee machine, the whirr of printers or the proximity to their bosses and colleagues.

At some point in our lives, many of us have experienced what happens when employees and teams become isolated from the larger whole, for one reason or another. For sure, in 2020 and 2021, a significant number of employees have experienced a sense of isolation, which may result in decreased productivity and negatively impact their well-being and mental health. It usually makes it harder for some individuals to engage with larger company goals and the greater purpose behind their work. Business leaders are facing the responsibility of mitigating workplace isolation and fostering social connections during unprecedented times of social distancing and remote work.

Key Lessons Learned from Remote Work

1. A FOCUS ON HEALTH, WELLNESS AND WELL-BEING IS BECOMING THE NEW NORMAL

Clearly, improving productivity is a key way to boost employee engagement and enhance company culture. That's why employee well-being isn't an issue that companies can afford to ignore. Workers who reported increased well-being were more productive and more likely to continue working at their current company, according to a 2019 meta-analysis by the Centre for Economic Performance at the London School of Economics and Political Science, as cited by SHRM. Notably, the research encompassed 339 independent studies in Gallup's database, reporting on 1.8 million employees in total. Interestingly, 68% of firms began one or more new wellness benefits during the pandemic, according to another survey conducted by Gartner.

2. INVESTING TIME AND EFFORT INTO VIRTUAL TEAM BUILDING IS CRUCIAL

Since working from home is here to stay, office parties and other employee appreciation events won't work in every situation. Neither will company-wide team-building retreats. Often, to foster cohesive teams, we need virtual games, challenges, or other activities that bond people together. Lots of options are available: social icebreakers, mystery games, competitions between teams, and more. That said, a specific activity may not necessarily be of paramount importance. What matters most is the increased sense of safety, trust, understanding and a sense of belonging that people feel when they bond and interact with their coworkers and peers. After all, the strongest teams are those that can carry out unified plans with confidence, not fear.

3. DEEPLY APPRECIATING EVERY TEAM MEMBER, REGARDLESS OF THEIR STATUS, IS A NECESSITY

Ultimately, the most engaged employees will be in the best position to consistently do their best and add value as they work towards accomplishing shared goals and fulfilling common values. No longer is employee appreciation just a water cooler buzzword. It's about valuing each person's knowledge, skills, and abilities, regardless of their position, status, or rank on the corporate ladder. When we can clearly see a path toward accomplishing something we believe in, and when we have a little fun along the way, then inspiration is almost inevitable.

3

COVID-19'S IMPACT ON ESSENTIAL WORKERS, WOMEN AND MINORITIES

Without a doubt, the global pandemic struck so instantly and unexpectedly, wreaking havoc all across our nation and catching us all off guard. It is important to note that the global disaster had a profound impact on some of the most vulnerable members of our society - minority groups, women, essential workers, and the elderly. It affected their health, working conditions and opportunities, and their day-to-day lives.

After an incredibly tough and stressful year, we developed a different outlook on so many things…and when it comes to our brave men and women working on the frontlines, we as a society developed a deeper appreciation for their courage, sacrifices and contribution, at a time when most people were 'hunkering" at home at the height of the pandemic.

Let's have a conversation about challenges, lessons learned and new ways to support those who were impacted the most.

Key Societal Challenges During the Pandemic

ESSENTIAL WORKERS STEPPING UP

While many governments around the world issued stay-at-home orders and imposed all kinds of restrictions intended to slow the spread of COVID-19, essential workers stepped up to the plate, demonstrating an indomitable spirit. We looked up to them and called them heroes as they fed us all, tended to our health, transported us, and performed so many other crucial tasks that held up our society. As soon as the crisis hit, they rolled up their sleeves and got to work, while facing increased exposure to the potentially deadly virus. Sadly, face coverings and other personal protective equipment were often in short supply, even in healthcare settings. This didn't stop them from taking care of others and risking their lives. Every single day.

In an effort to improve working conditions, some essential workers staged walkouts at companies like Instacart and Amazon, and at poultry processing plants. Slowly, many workplaces adapted, with enhanced leave policies and improved access to much-needed personal protective equipment. To show their support, some companies, including Kroger Company, Amazon, Walmart, and Target, offered bonuses or temporary pay increases while stay-at-home orders were in place.

"They can't see you right now—would you like a bottle while you're waiting?"

THE CHILDCARE BREAKDOWN

As schooling and childcare infrastructure utterly collapsed during the pandemic, employers and employees alike had to scramble to adapt. Some essential workers had some limited childcare options not available to other workers, such as district-sponsored programs. In general, however, many working parents had to care for children at home or rely on grandparents, other family members, or private nannies.

In the beginning, most people accepted the many work disruptions parents faced, including unexpected school closures and rather frustrating meeting interruptions by children. In some ways, these disruptions brought us all together as we collectively faced the unprecedented hardships caused by the pandemic or peeked into our coworkers' personal lives during Zoom meetings. Yet, this high level of tolerance was not to last.

Let's face it: all day every day, as exhausted parents juggled homeschooling and odd school hours, home technology and space considerations, emotional needs of the family, and so much more, something had to give. According to the U.S.

Census Bureau Household Pulse Survey, Week 12, from July 16-21, 2020, 25.3% of women and 9.9% of men, ages 18-64, reported not working due to childcare disruptions. Now that you know that about one-fifth of adults under 65 opted out of the workforce in favor of childcare, or were forced to, you can well imagine how many working parents lost hours and hours of productivity, due to increased household duties and constant distractions.

UNEQUAL IMPACTS OF DISASTER

Sadly, research suggests that minority groups bore the brunt of the pandemic's health impacts. In April, May, and June of 2020, Black and Hispanic patients made up 48.6% of COVID-19 hospitalizations, while hospitalizations for white patients represented only 38.8% of the total, according to the Agency for Healthcare Research and Quality (AHRQ)'s Healthcare Cost and Utilization Project. Behind these numbers are so many touching stories, individual lives, and families in crisis…

As a group, women have suffered, too. In December 2020, women accounted for 90% of the jobs lost, and 54% of the total jobs lost since the start of the pandemic, according to ABC News. Additionally, women's workforce participation will likely not recover until 2024, two years later than the estimated recovery time for men. These staggering numbers represent the many women who sacrificed jobs, careers, and some of their biggest dreams, to care for their children.

Furthermore, according to SWHR.org, women of color in particular were impacted the most by the devastating health crisis. As a result of deeply ingrained inequalities that are still prevalent in our society, they face even bigger challenges associated with both their gender and race. The sad truth is, women of color are more likely to live in poverty and are overrepresented in the industries hit the hardest by Covid-19 (such as hospitality and childcare). Many of them have lost their jobs, while those who are still employed don't have the luxury of working from home and enjoying the safety and flexibility of newly-created workplace arrangements.

For sure, the impact of all these challenges cannot be overstated. Yet, we can draw out some important, positive lessons that will help us move forward.

Key Lessons Learned: The Three C's of Lending a Hand and Making a Difference

1. CHILDCARE RAISES PRODUCTIVITY AMONG WORKING WOMEN

When we effectively manage childcare challenges, parents gain more time and energy to devote to their work. In 2019, the Council for a Strong America estimated that employers lose $13 billion in potential productivity and earnings, due to insufficient childcare resources. Notably, to begin to address this issue, some employers have considered backup childcare or childcare concierge services to help workers locate the right provider to meet their needs. For example, Target has offered free backup childcare to all of its U.S. workers through childcare provider Bright Horizons.

I believe that together, we will continue to explore a wide variety of solutions allowing parents to maintain productive jobs, knowing that their kids are in good hands and being taken care of during working hours.

2. CONVERSATIONS UNFOLDING AMONG LEADERS ON NEW POLICIES

New strategies, policies, and laws are in the works to better support women, people of color, low-wage employees, and essential workers. Among them are proposed new policies out of President Biden's White House that would increase attention on enhanced labor laws, higher wages, and employee classification issues. Biden has also advanced the proposed Protecting the Right to Organize (PRO) Act, which establishes penalties for companies that interfere with workers' organizing efforts by firing or otherwise retaliating against employees.

On April 26, 2021, President Biden established the White House Task Force on Worker Organizing and Empowerment, which was set to put forth recommendations for government action within 180 days. On April 27, by executive order, Biden raised the minimum wage for federal contractors to $15 per hour, going into effect in January 2022. Although the full effects of these policies on our economy remain to be seen, the White House believes that increasing the minimum wage will reduce turnover, lower recruitment costs, and increase worker productivity.

In support of his American Jobs Plan, President Biden also has put forth the Build Back Better initiative, which includes a $1.2 trillion Bipartisan Infrastructure Framework, similar to the New Deal passed under the Roosevelt administration.

According to Forbes, President Biden intends to create millions of employment opportunities with his new plan, citing estimates of up to $18 million jobs. In addition, he outlined a $2 trillion plan to rebuild infrastructure and rebuild the U.S. economy. If passed, this bill would be the largest ever federal transit investment and the largest ever electric vehicle (EV) infrastructure investment in the history of the U.S.

Of course, some of the proposed policy changes are controversial and are not supported by all business organizations. In the end, there is likely to be a balancing of interests that allows policies to move forward – the policies that support and advance the goals of working Americans, in concert with the businesses that create and supply the jobs.

3. COMPASSION GOES A LONG WAY IN TROUBLED TIMES

Each and every one of us can do our part to respond to these larger issues. It goes without saying that helping our colleagues overcome their challenges can be overwhelming, on top of our own. Yet, when we stop the rat race to step into their shoes for a moment, we are on our way to moving mountains. To assist someone who is struggling, the first step is often taking the time to listen and understand the challenge. Once we all begin to do that, we bring ourselves closer to a workable solution for everyone involved.

In conclusion, my sincere hope is that rather than slipping entirely back to the way things used to be, we will all continue to discuss issues facing women, minorities, and essential workers with respect, creativity, and an open mind.

4

THE RISING WAVE OF EMPLOYEE ACTIVISM

Now that employee activism is becoming more prevalent in the workplace, let me start off this chapter by briefly defining this concept. Simply put, Employee Activism is associated with actions that workers take to address specific events or company's policies and practices.

Evidence suggests that, over the last decade, employees have come together to take a passionate stand for what they believe is right, attempting to reverse what they perceive to be unfair business practices by influencing their employers. While activism is NOT a novel concept, things certainly came to a head in 2020 and 2021, with many workers feeling more empowered to make a difference. As the devastating pandemic reared its head and spread rapidly across our country, employees took center stage demanding change, accountability and justice, and raising the bar higher for organizations.

Without a doubt, these "change agents" show no signs of slowing down. In fact, more than 80% of employers expect their employees to become more engaged in activism by 2024, according to research by global law firm Herbert Smith Freehills, as cited by SHRM. In 2017, more than 70% of GenZ employees surveyed by Cone Communications indicated that working for a company that shares their values, passions, and concerns was highly important to them.

By 2019, employees at big companies were already actively protesting policies that affected the way their employers managed and addressed complex social issues. For instance, with a petition at Google and a walkout at Wayfair, workers voiced their concerns and spoke their minds on company policies affecting immigrants.

Then came the many stressors of the 2020 pandemic and the highly- publicized death of George Floyd. These historic events gave rise to a new wave of racial, social, and political unrest impacting workplaces, nationwide.

One widely-reported example involved game developer Activision Blizzard. In the summer of 2021, hundreds of employees organized a walkout and signed a letter to management expressing discontent over the company's alleged inadequate response to sexual harassment allegations brought by the California Department of Fair Employment and Housing. Reports suggest that while company spokespeople called the suit's claims of rampant harassment and discrimination "distorted," "insulting," and "irresponsible," employees spoke of their own personal experiences on social media. In the wake of the firestorm unfolding at the company, Blizzard's president eventually stepped down.

While these events have shed light on many important issues remaining in the workplace, they also have played a role in raising public awareness about some, arguably, "uncomfortable truths" that may not have been at the center of corporate discussions in the past.

Let's review some of the challenges that have arisen and the lessons we've learned in tumultuous times.

Issues, Challenges and Controversies Sweeping the Nation

RESPONDING TO ESSENTIAL WORKER STRIKES AND PROTESTS

Although organized worker movements occur annually on International Workers' Day (which is typically targeted toward unionized workers or those workers seeking to unionize), in some ways, 2020 was unprecedented. The Guardian reported that hundreds of essential workers at Walmart, Target, Amazon, Whole Foods, Shipt, and Instacart called in sick as part of a coordinated, nationwide strike to protest what they believed to be unsafe working conditions during the pandemic. Notably, 2020 International Workers' Day coincided with an end to stay-at-home orders in many states.

While some companies started implementing new safety measures and offering bonuses, some of their workers wanted more. According to multiple findings, essential workers faced increased exposure to COVID-19 right from the start, putting their health and lives at risk while serving others. Sadly, according to metrics cited by the CDC in an April 2021 report, in the state of California, alone, working-aged people's mortality risk (measured between March and October of 2020) increased 22%, when compared to their risk before the pandemic. Furthermore, reports suggest that Latino and Black Americans experienced the greatest increased mortality risk.

EMBRACING DIVERSITY

Today's business leaders and executives are facing the challenge of maintaining well-functioning, motivated and cohesive teams while effectively reconciling the differences in a diverse workplace. In addition, if they encourage diversity within their organizations, they may need to find ways to educate all employees about the benefits and positive characteristics that a diverse and inclusive workplace brings with it.

Another challenge is to help diverse teams find some common ground which may bring employees closer together and make it easier to collaborate and strive for common goals. Potential solutions include professionally-facilitated group discussions, affinity group sessions, guest speakers, reading clubs, or various volunteer opportunities.

Harvard Business Review has cited multiple studies showing that diverse groups and teams may lead to more accurate group thinking for organizations. Additionally, according to a study published by McKinsey entitled, "Why Diversity Matters," there is a significant correlation between diversity and financial performance. In fact, companies with greater ethnic and racial diversity among their staff performed up to 35% better than organizations "whose staff demographics matched the national average."

Another interesting observation, stated by McKinsey, is that companies with greater gender diversity performed 15% better than "companies with less gender diversity." A recent finding by the Boston Consulting Group has found that diversity among management not only increases the bottom line and improves financial performance, but also leads to increased innovation by more than 19%.

Key Lessons Learned

1. PROTECT REPUTATION BY CONSTRUCTIVELY LEVERAGING EMPLOYEE PASSIONS AND ACTIONS

The way a company reacts to employee voices and needs can bolster or taint its reputation. Take Limeade's CEO, Henry Albrecht, who told SHRM that the company's employee resource groups led to "a rich, positive leadership and board discussion." As a result, the company was able to enhance its recruiting and hiring practices and attract strong job candidates. In general, the ideal approach to DEI is a strategic, well-thought-out and meaningful plan, overseen by someone with authority to successfully implement company-wide changes.

2. THE IMPORTANCE OF PROACTIVELY ADDRESSING CONFLICT THROUGH HONEST DIALOGUE

When accusations fly and people start blaming one another, maintaining morale can be difficult. Perhaps one of the most challenging issues confronting employers is navigating potential workplace conflicts that may arise - especially in times of ambiguity and crisis. Yet, proactive conflict prevention is key to lasting success. Revisiting the employee handbook can effectively set the tone, reiterating a zero-tolerance stance toward inappropriate behavior.

Of course, unconscious biases and heightened emotions are only natural, especially in these difficult times. Fortunately, updated employee training by an experienced trainer and facilitator can reduce or prevent workplace discrimination and harassment, and it might even transform the workplace as a whole. This is especially true if the training allows employees to actively practice effective strategies to address biases and manage workplace emotions. If complaints arise, the best course of action is to immediately investigate and take any necessary remedial steps.

3. ADDRESSING THE THREE A'S: ALLEVIATING A SENSE OF ANXIETY, APPREHENSION AND ANGER

2020 and 2021 have been traumatizing years for many people, and especially people of color. Opting out of the conversation may be similar to ignoring the elephant in the room. Instead, as a society, we are learning to choose our responses with care and become more cognizant of the larger world outside the workplace.

An excellent first step is acknowledging employees' thoughts and emotions, so they feel heard and appreciated. A professional mediator can hold voluntary, 60-90-minute group listening sessions where employees may openly communicate their fears and concerns and discuss how current events impact them personally. Compassionate listening and understanding can restore a healthier mindset while positively impacting employee performance.

4. NEW HIRING PRACTICES: FROM TALKING THE TALK TO WALKING THE WALK

In 2020, alongside Black Lives Matter protests, employees have called employers out on what they considered to be insincere messaging around diversity. Social media hashtags such as #PullUpOrShutUp went viral revealing internal hiring practices. According to Microsoft's 2019 diversity and inclusion report, as cited by The Associated Press, less than 3% of its U.S. executives, managers, and directors, along with just 4.4% of its global workforce, identified as Black. Microsoft responded by pledging to strengthen connections with historically Black colleges and universities. Meanwhile, Adidas North America responded to their employees by announcing a planned $120 million investment in Black communities over the next four years, as well as promising to hire more Black and Hispanic employees to fill 30% of new Adidas and Reebok positions.

In December of 2020, four, high-level executives and one former CEO of IBM, Merck, Recognize, General Catalyst, and Amgen co-founded OneTen, a coalition of highly-influential business leaders coming together to "upskill, hire and promote one million Black Americans over the next 10 years into family-sustaining jobs with opportunities for advancement," according to the coalition's press release. The new alliance connects employers with "talent partners, leading nonprofits and other skill-credentialing organizations" that place high value on diversity.

2020 and 2021 are finally behind us and to date, 2022 continues to present many of the same challenges. A lot has been accomplished, and critical issues have finally come to light over the course of this highly-stressful and unprecedented year. In 2021, many workers were still engaged in activism, with a 20-day strike by Frito-Lay employees protesting 84-hour work weeks, and a nationwide strike by workers at Uber and Lyft, according to CBS News.

From local protests to global movements to internal complaints, employees are changing their relationships with their employers and feeling more empowered. In turn, employers are increasingly treating diversity, equity, and inclusion and other factors as crucial values to be nurtured throughout the organization. The most successful employers will be those who ensure their mission and values are aligned with both their internal and external presence and live up to those values in the eyes of their employees, investors, and other stakeholders.

'Ah, noise, people, traffic. I missed this.'

5

DAILY COMMUTE NO MORE? AVOIDING THE GRIND AND ESCAPING RUSH HOUR TRAFFIC

As the global pandemic, unexpectedly, descended on the world, it instantly changed the way most people work. At the height of the pandemic, a whopping 61% of employees ended up working remotely, 53% of whom had transitioned to working from home since COVID-19's onset, according to Salesforce research. By March 2021, it was clear that remote work and other flexible working arrangements are here to stay, probably for the long-term.

A survey conducted by the HR consultancy, Mercer, showed that 87% of its 700 employer respondents anticipated workplace flexibility as part of their post-pandemic strategy, with the majority embracing a hybrid model that requires less time at the office. And really, why wouldn't they? An employee working a half-time remote schedule saves the employer an estimated $11,000, according to Global Workplace Analytics.

With the way things turned out, we can't help but wonder: how many people working from home have been missing their daily commutes? After all, who loves the stress of driving in traffic, rushing to catch a bus, or getting stuck on the train?

Interestingly, data compiled by the University of Chicago, from 10,000 workers, showed a combined commuter savings of 62.4 million hours per day.

Now, you might be wondering, what do people do with their reclaimed time? Well, according to the data, they gave more than a third of that time back to their main job, and they spent about a third of that on childcare, outdoor recreation, and a second job, combined. Clearly, childcare needs cannot be ignored, and we will revisit them later in this book.

For now, let's talk about how some innovative companies have been managing common remote workplace concerns.

Key Challenges of Remote Work

Productivity versus Work/Life Balance

The pandemic has upended work, as we know it, blurring the lines between work and personal time and shedding a bright light on our perceptions of productivity. For instance, rather than making a good impression by spending long hours in the office, many professionals feel an increased need to check email or respond to messages throughout the day, making themselves available nearly 24/7. In fact, according to Microsoft's Work Trend Index survey from January 2021, 50% of people reply to Microsoft Teams chats within five short minutes.

Do you have your colleagues' personal cell phone numbers, and have you ever texted at least one of them, about a work issue during off-hours? Hard to believe that "back in the day," we were not texting our coworkers after work and had the luxury of spending quality time with our loved ones and friends.

Let's take a quick look at Slack and Buffer, two inspiring companies setting a great example for others:

Once upon a time, the collaboration and chat platform, Slack, was mainly designed for geeks. Not anymore. In fact, 65 Fortune 100 companies use Slack, according to the company's website. With instant communication constantly at our fingertips, setting boundaries and managing expectations is more important than ever. Notably, some companies are stepping up by empowering personnel at all levels to follow suit.

Buffer, the organization behind the popular social media scheduling tool, has personnel across 50 cities actively using Slack. To encourage employees to "get the most out of Slack while keeping our personal time our own," the company implemented what they call "*The 10 Slack Agreements of Buffer*".

These agreements establish norms and set boundaries, encouraging people to take downtime and display it on their statuses so that everyone will know, exactly when, to expect a response. "Focus zones" are also crucial, as is avoiding the constant checking of messages. In addition, the agreements include a general guideline to respond to direct messages by the end of the workday.

STRENGTHENING RAPPORT AMONG REMOTE WORKERS

While too much traditional water cooler talk could be distracting, it goes without saying that face time with colleagues and leaders is a key strategy for deepening relationships and vying for promotions, as well as gaining access to other opportunities with companies. As Zoom replaced these key interactions, we found we could be more "ourselves" in the face of a shared crisis. As we are, collectively, struggling through the devastating pandemic, sometimes we can take a quick peek into each other's homes and family lives, observe raw emotions, or even get a glimpse of adorable kids running around, funny pets, and household objects.

Yet, in our brave new virtual world, Zoom fatigue is no mere catchphrase, and workers unaccustomed to so much camera time and remote interactions, have longed to return to their offices to get back into the swing of things. People are craving more creative ways to connect, and I believe that, both virtual and in-person team-building, will help fill that niche.

Can little nudges, every now and then, help you genuinely connect with coworkers? The folks at Hunu think we certainly can, as suggested by Yale Insights. Founded by former Google executives, Hunu's artificial intelligence urges employees to create little moments of connection: speaking up at a meeting, praising a co-worker's achievements, or asking for input or feedback, among other things. Eventually, following these carefully - timed cues can potentially make a big difference in how we connect, collaborate, and interact with one another. Once we make connection "the norm," we will be better equipped to build what Hunu calls "psychological safety" to establish team spirit and trust.

MAXIMIZING POTENTIAL: MANAGING EMPLOYEES REMOTELY

How many managers have ever been trained to work with remote teams? As an experienced employment attorney and mediator, I can tell the difference between managers who received adequate training, and those who have not. In this new frontier, training is crucial because even the best, smartest, and most capable team members are expected to learn, grow, and evolve to be able to bring greater value to their organization.

As early as 2015, Harvard Business Review asked over 1100 people to describe someone "especially good at managing remote teams." 46% of the 800 respondents mentioned frequent and consistent check-ins as a savvy strategy to engage employees and keep everyone on the same page. In other words, scheduled, one-on-one Zoom meetings, regular emails, phone calls, or other consistent forms of remote interaction can make a difference and improve morale.

Many other responses revolved around designating team time for personal interactions and nurturing relationships. As the saying goes, "there is more to life than the daily grind." For example, going beyond daily work responsibilities and taking the time to learn more about your colleagues, their interests, hobbies, and families is usually time well-spent, which may result in deeper relationships and improved productivity.

Considering that some employees may get more office time than others, it is vital to make every single individual feel included and indispensable, regardless of location.

Key Lessons Learned from Remote Work

1. Flexibility Matters: Hybrid Model Optimal for Many

Interestingly, Microsoft has called the hybrid model of work "the next great disruption."

An early trend toward this model has been a surprise to some and a no-brainer to others. While workers are thrilled to return to their office lives and resume daily "watercooler gatherings," many employees developed a deeper appreciation for the flexibility that remote work provides. Whether it is working from home, one day a week, or changing the number of hours spent in the office each day, most people love the freedom to choose how they live their lives. Therefore, the changes brought on by COVID-19 can lead to a more balanced and satisfying lifestyle and positively influence employee productivity.

"It's just me today. Everyone else is working remotely."

2. BEING ON SITE, STILL CRITICAL, FOR MANY SERVICE-BASED AND MANUFACTURING JOBS

Notably, COVID-19 taught us there are many jobs that can't be done from home. According to Stanford Economist Nicholas Bloom, who conducted nationwide surveys in 2020, 51% of survey respondents said they were able to work from home at 80% efficiency or higher. These people were mostly professionals, managers, and financial workers using computers. The remaining respondents represented the retail, healthcare, business services, and transportation sectors. It goes without saying that customer - facing jobs or those requiring heavy equipment are especially suited to on-site work and cannot be performed remotely.

IMPACT ON PRODUCTIVITY: THE IDEA OF WORKING HARD AND PLAYING HARD

Evidence suggests that how we feel affects how we work. If you have ever felt terrible after spending a long time at one task, or if you have ever felt recharged and invigorated after a vacation, then you have experienced the highs and lows of your work/life balance habits. Come to think of it…how many employees enjoy the newly-found opportunity to spend more time with their kids, help them with their homework, or take them to a doctor? Even being able to drop by their parents' house and check on their well-being can be very gratifying.

Those who feel stressed or overwhelmed, now have the freedom to take a longer break, take a walk in the park, or engage in a quick exercise routine, which was previously impossible when they had to be at the office all day, every day.

In conclusion, one major silver lining of the pandemic is that many employees now have the flexibility to enjoy a greater work/life balance, which will certainly impact workplace productivity. I am optimistic about the future, as forward-thinking companies utilize new technologies, tried-and-true strategies, a little common sense, and a lot of heart to move us through this pivotal work transition.

6

THE IMPORTANCE OF DISASTER PREPAREDNESS AND CRISIS PREVENTION

It goes without saying that the COVID-19 pandemic left many employers scrambling to survive or stay afloat. While many businesses and nonprofits may have planned for certain contingencies, their efforts did not prepare them for the staggering amount of change caused by the global disaster. Decreased revenue, safety concerns, and a new pandemic-driven business landscape accelerated these transformations. Additionally, facing the myriad of devastating effects of the virus has shifted our focus toward crisis management and prevention, urging us to develop specific well-thought-out plans for potential calamities.

Challenges and Adaptations

TACKLING OPERATIONAL CHANGES

The pandemic, and all of its closures, led to supply chain disruptions, dramatic changes in market forces, increased safety concerns, and many other factors affecting business operations. Naturally, leaders of businesses and nonprofits, everywhere, faced difficult operational choices. They had to tackle conflicting priorities: cutting costs, managing cash-flow, shifting to remote work when feasible, ramping-up security, or maintaining a safe working environment with personal protective equipment and social distancing.

As companies laid off or furloughed workers, reduced employees' hours, and cut employee compensation, they did what they could to minimize disruptions and maintain excellent customer service. In an effort to explain why some organizations performed better than others while keeping costs down, Gartner analyzed 2020 earnings-call transcripts among S&P 500 companies. The analysis showed that the best performers implemented early cost-savings measures while investing in their employees during the same year. Top employee investments included benefits initiatives and other crucial health and well-being programs.

MAINTAINING MORALE IN UNCERTAIN TIMES

Clearly, with all these new changes and future unknowns, many employees were more worried, stressed and distracted than usual on the job. It comes as no surprise that the added job stressors decreased morale for so many workers, who were already struggling to manage their families' physical and mental health in the middle of the global crisis.

Although managers often feel powerless to maintain company morale after making difficult decisions, it is possible to make things a bit easier for team members. Clear, heartfelt and transparent communication about the reason for the decision goes a long way, as does honest employee reassurances about the company's future. In addition, employees usually feel relieved knowing that major changes are finally over.

For workers who have been laid off, well-managed job placement, exit coaching or career transition services can make all the difference in the world, soften the blow and offer hope. If feasible, maintaining crucial health benefits provides some stability and decreases enormous anxiety or a sense of helplessness caused by a sudden job loss.

CREATING SECURE, AD-HOC TECH SOLUTIONS

Unfortunately, with the onset of COVID, many people had to flounder on their own as they were trying to figure out how to navigate unfamiliar software, poor or slow internet connections, and fewer resources to do their jobs from home. Additionally, while cybersecurity is essential for anyone using the Internet, remote workers may be facing serious cybersecurity threats and all kinds of other technology challenges.

For instance, when suddenly told they could no longer come to work every day, many people started accessing confidential data using an unsecured wireless home network or personal device. It is important to keep in mind that too many consumer-grade or personal devices aren't properly updated or protected, leaving them vulnerable to all sorts of exploits. Yet, in the middle of a stay-at-home order or other unexpected crisis that limits employees' ability to work at the office, it is all too easy to attempt such ad-hoc solutions with major security flaws.

Topping it all off, remote employees often needed to use these solutions without adequate support from an experienced IT professional, while still remaining productive. According to cybersecurity firm Tessian, as cited in a May 2020 ZDNet article, half of its survey respondents reported the need to work around their company's security policies to efficiently do their jobs.

Now, as we recover and learn to better address these challenges, we can take away some crucial lessons. After all, one of the best ways we can respond to a crisis is to find new opportunities for growth.

Key Lessons Learned: Plan, Train and Upgrade

1. PLANNING AHEAD: NECESSITY OF CRISIS PREVENTION

To ensure adequate infrastructure, business continuity, and high employee safety standards, both prevention and action are key. All too often, companies pay lip service to crisis prevention or action plans. Let's face it: We have all experienced, first-hand, some of the worst of what can happen; now is the time to move forward so that everyone, at every level, is held accountable for creating and maintaining the above standards.

One way to achieve this is to create teams of highly-involved personnel, whose input and feedback is respected by qualified team leads.

Upon researching and assessing risks, the strongest companies create or update plans to meet various needs. For instance, we can all create plans to prevent illness or injury in a variety of circumstances, from public health emergencies to natural disasters to workplace violence. We should also ensure that the appropriate safety equipment is in the budget and that we have time for the requisite safety checks and drills. While the timing and purpose of these checks and drills may vary, an annual overview is a good rule of thumb. Furthermore, we cannot afford to underestimate the value of experienced consultants and the knowledge they bring to the table as we make difficult decisions about complex issues and attempt to predict the future.

2. EFFECTIVE TRAINING KEY TO CRISIS MANAGEMENT

When it comes to crisis management, effective communications are critical. To panic is all too human, so we must instruct and empower every employee with the skills they need to respond to emergencies. Each type of crisis may have different people managing different aspects of the situation. Effective planning typically helps companies address challenges before they evolve into crises. Well-thought-out crisis management strategies also make a company a more desirable place to work, improve its reputation, and minimize potential damages.

3. TECHNOLOGY UPGRADES KEEP BUSINESS FLOWING

Data and intellectual property are often a business's most valuable assets. That's why it behooves any organization to empower its people with technology and training, allowing both remote and on-site workers to resolve unexpected situations without letting down their guard. While remote work has become the norm, outdated or misconfigured technology can potentially wreak havoc on a business.

Fortunately, in addition to essential maintenance and upgrades, ZDNet recommended ways to beef up security and infrastructure for remote workers. These steps include replacing simple user IDs and passwords with multi-factor authentication, as well as properly configuring the company's virtual private network (VPN), which is an encrypted connection.

In conclusion, let's allow the pandemic to serve as the impetus to boost our resilience by planning for future crises, whether they relate to health, weather, nature, terrorism, workplace violence, or other disasters. When we plan, train, and practice, we can truly overcome.

7

DISCERNING LEGAL CHALLENGES AND CHANGES

Without a doubt, change has been the name of the game in 2020 and 2021, and it continues to unfold and influence every aspect of our lives. Our system of laws and regulations is no exception, since the pandemic has created new legal challenges and has led to a closer examination of existing ones.

As a former employment litigation attorney turned mediator, arbitrator, and investigator, I could have easily written a long chapter chock full of confusing details and legalese that many readers would probably put aside. Instead, I decided that I would focus on how some of the legal issues of this past year have impacted the workplace, while we are still grappling with rapid change. Valuable lessons gleaned from these touchy issues lead us to some tried-and-true insights that can help, both employers and employees, navigate this evolving legal landscape.

Legal Controversies

LAYOFFS AND TERMINATIONS

In July 2021, as cited by AARP Public Policy Institute's Employment Data Digest, 51.6% of jobseekers ages 55 and older were considered "long-term unemployed" by the U.S. Bureau of Labor Statistics, compared to 34.8% of jobseekers ages 16-54. Could discriminatory hiring or firing practices be a contributing factor in America?

In my own experience as a mediator, I've seen more sessions during the pandemic in which a terminated employee alleges discrimination based on age or race, whereas the employer asserts that the termination was part of a legitimate, pandemic-related, cost-saving measure. The key legal question in such situations is whether the employer's true reason for the alleged wrongful termination was based on economic and other business reasons, or was it a guise to get rid of an employee who the employer believed to be low-performing or no longer an asset to the organization? These cases turn on the underlying facts and issues surrounding the layoff or termination.

THE CHANGING NATURE OF HARASSMENT AND DISCRIMINATION IN THE WORKPLACE

Now that quite a few of us are working remotely from home, some people may mistakenly assume that harassment is a thing of the past, and there is no need to address or worry about this issue in times like these. After all, how can you possibly bother someone who is no longer sharing an office space with you, right? Well…believe it or not, nothing could be further from the truth.

While physical harassment may have declined for those who transitioned to working from home, sadly, other forms of provocation transitioned online. When Deloitte surveyed 5,000 working women across 10 countries, the data showed that 52% had experienced harassment or microaggressions of some sort over this past pandemic year, as cited by *The New York Times*. In a nutshell, workplace harassment occurs when an employee or an employer deliberately or unconsciously targets those who possess certain legally-protected characteristics (such as gender, race, color, national origin, religion, familial status, age, etc.) and behaves in a way that belittles, disempowers, or even threatens these individuals.

Although most of us spend our workdays behind a computer screen at home, surprisingly, there has been no shortage in claims of online sexual harassment, racist jokes, or homophobic slurs permeating our virtual workplaces. Indeed, conduct that might be considered "micro-aggressive" has seen an increase these past two years. Discussed above, microaggressions are small, often unintended actions that the recipient can easily interpret as personal slights against a marginalized racial, cultural, or other group to which they belong. As many of us traded professional offices for webcams in our homes, the way people commit microaggressions has changed, too. For example, an employee might negatively judge a woman based on her hairstyle or how she is dressed, critique a religious decoration or arrangement in someone's home office, or routinely question a woman's views more than a man's during Zoom meetings.

It goes without saying that intentionally - damaging or cruel online actions can taint the reputation of a business or derail a career, no matter how "illustrious." Ken Kurson's story serves as an example of the alleged online behavior that may result in devastating consequences and ruin a person's professional standing.

In August 2021, a New York State prosecutor filed charges related to cyberstalking against Mr. Kurson, the former editor of *The New York Observer*. The allegations included eavesdropping and computer trespassing, both which are types of cybercrimes. According to the Wall Street Journal, he used an electronic monitoring software program, commonly known as spyware, to monitor his wife's keystrokes, obtained her passwords and accessed her Facebook and Gmail accounts. Previously, in October of 2020, federal prosecutors had hit him with similar charges pertaining to cyberstalking three victims. "Kurson used multiple aliases to file false complaints about two of the victims with their employer, post false negative reviews about one victim's professional conduct on crowd-sourced review websites, and made unsolicited contact with two of the victims," federal prosecutors said in a statement reported by NBC News.

RAISING QUESTIONS ABOUT VACCINES: TO MANDATE OR NOT TO MANDATE

For many, the increase in cases of the highly - contagious Delta variant has brought a sense of urgency to this important question. Did you know that in 1905, the U.S. Supreme Court upheld a state's power to mandate vaccination and fine people for noncompliance? Back then, it was smallpox. Now, it's COVID-19. In 2021, New York City and San Francisco became the first cities to mandate vaccinations as a prerequisite for participating in many indoor activities, with plenty of pushback from business owners and the general public.

Let's face it: For a company, creating an internal vaccination policy is no easy feat, with all the opinions circulating among the public. Even though the U.S. Equal Employment Opportunity Commission deemed mandatory vaccinations legal at work, employers are still treading in uncharted waters as they carefully examine, manage, and monitor the pros, cons, and legal exceptions that are part of the process. Naturally, they are facing the challenge of balancing individual needs, including medical conditions or religious beliefs, against the needs of the company as a whole.

Unsurprisingly, many hospitals and healthcare systems are implementing their own vaccination mandates. By mid-August, nine states had already announced some level of vaccination requirements for healthcare workers, according to Becker's Hospital Review. Other organizations unrelated to healthcare, from Walmart to Disney, are doing the same as they consider bringing more employees back to the workplace. In explaining Disney's policy that applies to all salaried and non-union workers, Disney CEO Bob Chapek told CNBC's Mad Money: "We believe what we'd like to do is convince them that it's in everyone's best interest in order to get vaccinated for the greater good... and the greater good includes our guests."

Key Lessons Learned

1. CONSIDER A COMPANY-WIDE REVIEW OF POLICIES

With all these changes, it may be a good idea to revisit the employee handbook and review the guidelines. Do its policies create a safe and welcoming environment? How are they going to impact productivity and employee morale in the new age of remote work and the #MeToo movement?

In response to the new workplace culture, harassment and social media policies have become commonplace in employee manuals everywhere. Additionally, we've seen the differences and similarities between in-office and remote workplace behavior. Therefore, many companies may benefit from upgraded and highly - detailed remote work policies that help employees function to the best of their ability (while away from the office).

2. UPDATED TRAINING NEEDED TO ADDRESS REPORTING REQUIREMENTS

Since more employees than ever before are working remotely, compliance with reporting requirements can be especially challenging. The question is, how do you handle inappropriate chat messages sent on a platform that does not save transcripts, for example? Or how are employees and managers documenting what goes on at the company in order to provide proof or avoid a wrongful termination claim? Given the circumstances, preparation is key. Organizations may want to take proactive steps to anticipate potential problems, ahead of time, and put a specific action plan into place.

Furthermore, for the system to work, employees need clear guidelines on how to report offensive behaviors, as well as who to contact and when. Those who handle reports at the organization may require specialized training to be able to effectively manage complaints, respond to emergencies, maintain accuracy, and remain sensitive to the needs of all parties involved - employees and employers, alike.

3. NEW CHANGES REQUIRE NEW WAYS OF ACCEPTING EMPLOYEE FEEDBACK

Encouraging timely reporting and feedback can improve both productivity and well-being of workers, as these vehicles of communication empower staff members to voice their concerns, resolve complaints and help them feel safe, both at the office and at home. For employees to confidently report an incident or provide feedback on a new policy, they must have reason to believe that they will be safe from potential retaliation. One possible solution is to establish an independent reporting hotline, managed by a third party. Calling this special phone number may be less intimidating than speaking to a supervisor or HR manager and may alleviate reluctance to speak up in a time of need.

In sum, we live in a climate of evolving laws and regulations that personally affect staff at every level of a company. Keeping up with so many changes can be time-consuming, stressful and overwhelming, to say the least. It's also easy to miss a tiny sentence, detail, or nuance in the law that may have a big impact. When in doubt, talk to HR. Also, an experienced employment attorney or mediator can help you remain compliant and address issues head-on.

CONCLUSION

"There are certain life lessons that you can only learn in the struggle."
- Idowu Koyenikan, Wealth for All

As I wrap up this book, this time capsule if you will, I can't help but feel inspired by how much society has adapted - in such a short period of time. Virtually overnight, we transformed the way we work in fundamental ways. Perhaps most importantly, the pandemic has created countless unsung heroes in workplaces all across our country and around the globe. In addition, as I stated throughout this book, there are so many lessons we have learned in less than two years and so many more to learn as we navigate the unknown. There are pointers to keep in mind and potential crises to foresee, prevent, or overcome successfully. One thing is for sure: something good comes along through adversity, and that's what happened as a result of the global health crisis.

Now, as we move forward into the future, let's reflect on a few major pointers that capture the essence of the pandemic and its influence on the way we will work and do business in our present and near future.

1. LEADERS MUST PAVE THE WAY

Naturally, management is key during any time of transition or upheaval. As conditions change, leaders have the power to strengthen or even redefine, in a very real and transparent way, a company's mission, values, and corporate culture, fostering long-term resilience. A new type of leader is rising up as well, and HR still has so much to figure out while taking on more responsibility. In fact, human resources professionals are particularly poised to step up the game and step out of their comfort zone as they address challenging situations impacting employee motivation, and transform challenges into new opportunities, which may ultimately raise the bar on the performance of the entire company.

2. EMPATHY AND COMMUNICATION ARE KEY TO CRISIS MANAGEMENT

It goes without saying that connection is key for employees at every level: connection to the larger mission, connection to each other, and a sense of belonging and being part of a team that is doing important work. Of course, this sense of solidarity does not happen overnight, and it can slip all too easily during tumultuous times. On the other hand, when handled well, crises unite people like nothing else ever could. Clear, transparent communication makes all the difference, from the top levels of an organization, down to the most recent entry-level hires. Open, empathetic discussion is at the foundation of any team-building effort, especially when diversity concerns are at play.

3. ADEQUATE PLANNING CANNOT BE UNDERESTIMATED

While the pandemic caught most of us completely off guard, it shed light on the many crises that we can predict, prepare for, or even prevent. From future health emergencies to weather-related disasters, and from childcare disruptions to technology woes, we can establish crisis prevention and crisis management plans. These plans clearly and efficiently assign the right responsibilities to the right people so that if the worst does happen, everyone can play their part and come out on top.

4. PERSONNEL RETRAINING IS THE NEXT STEP FOR MANY

As we manage the ongoing pandemic, and well beyond, we find ourselves in a different place than we were before. As we review and revise existing crisis management and prevention plans, it may be time to retrain managers and employees on evolving expectations. It may sound simplistic, but clear, well-articulated procedures and guidelines have a major impact in reducing stress, conflict, and human error.

FINAL WORDS

Even as we still grapple with waves of a seemingly unceasing pandemic, we can reflect on the powerful insights we can gain from these comparatively brief moments in human history, both as individuals and as a society. Let's view these crucial lessons as stepping stones from which to leap forward: from a time of crisis into a brighter, safer, and thriving future.

ACKNOWLEDGMENTS

I would be remiss if I did not take this opportunity to thank those who have made and continue to make it possible for me to be who I am and to do the work that I do daily.

First, I am grateful beyond measure to my family and friends for their unwavering love and support, including my mom Wilma *(the wind beneath my wings)*, my dad Cornelius, Jr. and bonus mom Joyce, my bonus/second parents – uncle Norman/Stanley and aunt Nadine (including the Ward and Frazier families), my husband, super supporter and cheerleader Steven E. (and the Wright family), my grandmother Sadie Mae, great aunt Bessie "Baby Sister," Birmingham aunts and "tees" Deborah, Toni, and Vicki, uncles Nathaniel, Jr. and Keith, brother Michael, and the rest of my wonderful family, near and far.

I also pay tribute to the memory of my grandmother Fletta Lucille, whose heart and spirit I inherited and strive to reflect each day. I also remember my grandfathers, Nathaniel, Sr. and Cornelius, Sr., my great grandmothers Arlena and Ira Bell, adopted grandparents Arthur and Opal, and other ancestors who have passed on, but whose legacies continue to motivate and inspire me in all that I do.

Many thanks to my closest friends and "framily" who sit on my front row and cheer me on – too many to name - I appreciate you all.

Additionally, I am grateful to my church family at Citizens of Zion Missionary Baptist Church of Compton, CA, including my current pastor Bobby Newman Jr. and his wife Lady Claudia, and my pastor of 40+ years who passed recently – Dr. Bobby T. Newman and his wife Lady Charmaine.

Special thanks to my hardworking team at the Reddock Law Group and my amazing colleagues at Judicate West. You all make it possible for me to work in a field that I love and am fortunate to be a part of.

Thank you to my clients, fellow attorney colleagues, and business associates who have supported my legal and ADR career for over twenty-five years. I am grateful to each of you and appreciate the opportunity to work with you. You have provided me a window seat to the ever evolving changes in the workplace, many of which serve as a basis for this book. For this I am thankful.

Many thanks to my friends and colleagues from the Southern California Mediation Association (SCMA), the Association of Workplace Investigators (AWI), the USC Gould School of Law and California State University Dominguez Hills mediation and peacemaking programs, the UCLA Extension business and human resources certification program, the Los Angeles County Equity Oversight Panel, and the Los Angeles World Airports. I am proud of the work we all do collectively to make a difference in the lives of people daily.

Thank you to my friends and colleagues from my member and associate bar associations and legal organizations, including the College of Labor & Employment Lawyers, the American Bar Association (ABA) Dispute Resolution Section, the National Bar Association (NBA) Commercial Law Section, the National Employment Law Council (NELC), the California Minority Corporate Counsel Program (CMCP), the California Association of Black Lawyers (CABL), the Los Angeles County

Bar Association (LACBA) Board of Trustees and Labor & Employment Law Section, the California Employment Lawyers Association (CELA), the Consumer Attorneys Association of Los Angeles (CAALA), the John M. Langston Bar Association, Black Women Lawyers Association of Los Angeles (BWL), and the Women Lawyers Association of Los Angeles (WLALA).

Thank you to my new colleagues at KBLA Talk 1580 radio, including founder and owner Tavis Smiley, the management team, the amazing daily and weekend hosts, engineers, and my production team – Irina, Myisha, Miles and Odale. Serving as the host of the weekly "Legal Lens with Angela Reddock-Wright" radio show has been one of the new joys of my life and professional career. I could not do it without each of you.

I am grateful for my friends and colleagues who work tirelessly to make a difference in our civic and community lives, including members of the Los Angeles African American Women's Public Policy Institute (LAAAWPPI), the Los Angeles Urban League, the International Black Women's Public Policy Institute (IBWPPI), Ability First, Women in Non-Traditional Employment Roles (WINTER), the California Black Women's Collective, the Los Angeles Chamber of Commerce, and the Young Invincibles, among others.

Last but not least, a big thanks to my publisher (Stephanie & Red Penguin Books), editors (Angela K., Krista and Pat), public relations team (Angela K., Lisa, Olivier, Cherie, KWSM, including Katie, Stephen, Jeff, Casey, Angie, and Monty, and Newsroom PR, including Howard, Brenda, Melissa and Terry), photography (Larry W. - book headshot and David H.), my glam squad (John - hair for book headshot, Procka/Patrice - make-up for book headshot, and make-up artist Elsie), social media team (Irina and Kaleidoscope Consulting, including Bonique and Nikki), graphics (Amy - book cover and other graphics, Serena & Carla).

I appreciate each person who helped me with the process of writing and publishing this book, a milestone I could not have achieved without each of you and your amazing talents.

Most importantly, I give ALL thanks to God, without whom I am nothing, and through whom, I move and have my being. ALL things are possible with and through Him. I am eternally grateful.

With Gratitude,
Angela

ABOUT THE AUTHOR

(Photo courtesy of Larry Warmsley Photography)

Named a "Best Lawyer in America" by U.S. News & World Report, a "Top 50 California Woman Attorney" by Super Lawyers, and a "Top California Employment Lawyer" by the Daily Journal, among other accolades, Angela Reddock-Wright is a distinguished employment and labor law attorney, turned alternative dispute resolution (ADR) professional, serving as a mediator, arbitrator, and workplace & Title IX investigator.

Reddock-Wright is the founder and managing partner of the Reddock Law Group, an employment mediation and dispute resolution firm based in Los Angeles, California serving clients both nationally and globally. She also serves on the distinguished panel of mediators and arbitrators with Judicate West, a private dispute resolution firm based in California.

With more than 25 years of legal experience, and in her role as a mediator and neutral, Reddock-Wright works with employers and employees to help them successfully resolve some of the most complex disputes that inevitably arise in the workplace, especially in the post COVID-19 world, the era of #MeToo, employee activism, and strides for racial, gender and other areas of equity and diversity. Reddock-Wright and her firm also are retained to conduct high-level workplace and Title IX investigations involving executives, management, elected officials, celebrity, and media personalities.

Well-regarded for her deep understanding of the workplace and the critical factors that contribute to a successful work environment, Reddock-Wright is also an established strategic human resources and diversity, equity, and inclusion (DEI) consultant and trainer, working with organizations to help them connect their mission, vision and values to the recruitment, retention, and growth of their most valued investment - their employees.

Reddock-Wright is a highly-sought-after media personality and legal analyst who is called upon to discuss a wide array of employment and workplace-related legal and other issues on major broadcast and print mediums, including ABC's Good Morning America and other ABC news shows and affiliates, Entertainment Tonight, CNN, MSNBC, BBC, Court TV,

NBC4, CBS2, KTLA5, NPR Radio, the New York Times, Washington Post, Los Angeles Times, USA Today, and People Magazine, among many others.

In October 2021, Reddock-Wright joined Tavis Smiley's KBLA Talk 1580 to host "Legal Lens With Angela Reddock-Wright," a popular weekend radio show where she "Brings Law to Light" by interviewing leading attorneys, legislative, and policy leaders to help educate, empower, and inspire listeners on trending issues shaping the legal and policy landscape today.

Reddock-Wright is a past president of the Southern California Mediation Association (SCMA) and is a volunteer mediator with the United States District Court – Central District. She also has served as an arbitrator and mediator with the American Arbitration Association and serves as an adjunct lecturer in the mediation programs at USC Gould School of Law and California State University, Dominguez Hills, as well as the Human Resources Certification program at UCLA Extension.

Recently elected to the distinguished College of Labor & Employment Lawyers, Reddock-Wright is a proud graduate of UCLA School of Law, Amherst College, the Coro Fellows' Program in Public Policy and Public Affairs, and the Brentwood School of Los Angeles. While in college, she had the opportunity to study abroad in the United Kingdom at Saint Catherine's College, Oxford University.

Reddock-Wright obtained her initial training as a mediator and neutral at the Straus Institute for Dispute Resolution at Pepperdine University School of Law. She also has had the privilege of traveling throughout Europe as a civic fellow with the German Marshall Memorial Fund, and to Israel with the Jewish Federation of Los Angeles.

Reddock-Wright is an author, public speaker, and blogger (www.angelareddock-wright.com), writing and speaking on the latest topics and trends in employment law, the workplace, mediation, arbitration, and investigations. She also serves as a board member for several non-profit and civic organizations and believes that "to whom much is given, much is required."

Reddock-Wright is passionate about the American and global workplace and has embraced as her life's work and mission to help employees and employers rise above the daily challenges they face to create healthy, dynamic, and thriving workplaces.

www.ingramcontent.com/pod-product-compliance
Lightning Source LLC
Chambersburg PA
CBHW071118030426
42336CB00013BA/2136